Kindle Fire HD Manual

The Ultimate Kindle Fire HD Guide for Beginners

by Amber Norato

Introduction

Back in 2011, the Amazon Kindle Fire came out with a bang (but not without its share of criticisms) and instantly became of the hottest holiday gifts of the year owing to its sleek, attractive design and the comparatively lower $159 price tag that went along with it.

In the fall of 2012, a survey by Forrester Research suggested that the Kindle Fire is second in sales only to Apple's iPad!

Now, you have the Kindle in high-definition. If you have already laid hands on the new device, we can help you navigate its features to help achieve the best user experience. If you have used the first-generation Kindle Fire, you will find the information laid out in this eBook easy to follow.

Unlike many Kindle Fire guides available on the Internet, we have been prudent to collate only those tips that will really benefit the users, instead of filling up pages with random information on the tablet. So instead of offering redundant tips like "how to charge the Kindle we

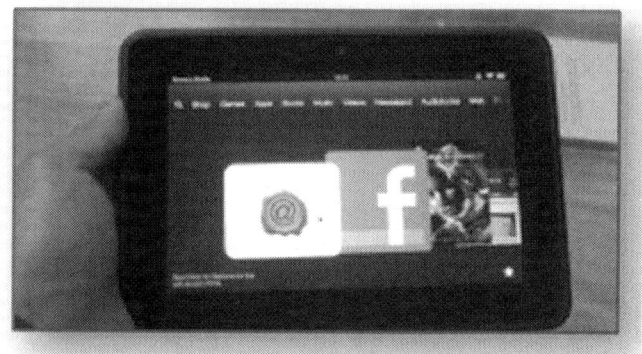

will advise on how to maximize the battery life.

Transition to HD

Here is a brief overview of major changes between the first-generation Kindle Fire and its HD successor. Most important of these changes relate to the design of the new Kindle Fire HD.

The first notable change with the Kindle Fire HD is that when you hold the device in the landscape mode (or as a movie screen), the audio will be played from speakers fitted on both sides of the device. In other words, you do not need headphones to watch movies in audio formats like Dolby Digital stereo.

In the initial version of the Kindle Fire, speakers were fitted on one side only, and even now the non-HD versions have the same design.

Moving on, Kindle Fire HD is out in 2 screen sizes; the 7" (1280x800 resolution) and the 8.9" (1920x1200 resolution), where as the models from the previous one have 1024x600 pixel screen. The new screens, coupled with the addition of micro HDMI bring you a new and improved movie watching experience on the tablet.

Finally, storage capacity has also increased on the HD models, ranging from 16 GB to 32 GB, and even going up to 64 GB on the 8.9" device. Previously you only had 8 GB of storage space.

Basic Tips

As the owner of a Kindle Fire HD, you have the privilege of using a device with a unique user interface. However, this also means that you will have to do some probing to find your way around the tablet. In this section, we will discuss the very basic tips of handling the Kindle Fire.

Kindle Fire HD Start-Up

This process hardly takes any time, and the device itself gives you a basic setup tour. However, you have to perform several functions yourself, such as selecting a main language (unless you know multiple languages). When asked, connect the tablet to a Wi-Fi network.

If the Kindle Fire HD is your very first tablet and you need some help in navigating the UI, you can always visit the help section at Amazon.

Here you will find articles and videos that help you find your way through the device.

You can visit the Amazon help page directly from the device. In addition, there is a "Help & Feedback" section in the settings menu which you will find in the start screen.

Securing the Device

Since you will use the Kindle for personal activities for the most part, what can be more basic (and yet useful) than setting up a lock screen password.

Simply go to "Settings" and enter "Security" found in the "More" section. To open the settings menu, swipe downwards from the top once the screen is unlocked. Turn the Lock screen password on to secure your device in case of any mishap. You can choose a PIN or a word password.

Note that if you forget the password, you have to reset the device to default factory settings to unlock it. This means all programs and applications on your device have to be downloaded all over again.

Switching to default settings will prove to be useful in a number of situations. For instance, if you are reselling the Kindle Fire HD or simply give it to someone, you will have to delete your personal files from the device.

In addition, if you have downloaded a lot of content, you may delete everything to free the memory. When you tap the "Erase Everything" option in the settings menu, you will see a confirm dialog box. You can proceed with the deletion procedure or tap "Cancel" in the dialog box if you change your mind.

Setting Up Your Accounts

Now is the time to sign into your Amazon account. If the device was purchased via your Amazon account, it will already be set up on the Kindle. On the other hand, if you received the

Kindle Fire HD as a present, you will have to change the Amazon account settings in order to regulate your online shopping from the device. Once you have chosen the correct time zone, finish the set-up by confirming the account.

After Amazon, the device may suggest that you set up your social networking accounts as well, such as Facebook and Twitter, in order to view and share updates. To sign in your Facebook or Twitter account, type the user name and password, but this procedure can always be skipped for another time.

Note that the ability of view updates on these websites requires you to download the specific apps. These can be downloaded from the Amazon App Store. This device enables you to swipe through apps, videos, and other programs in a carousel on the main screen (more on this below).

To set up your Twitter and Facebook accounts on the Kindle, bring the notifications bar into view by scrolling down from the top of the screen. Tap "Select" followed by "More. Now hit the option "Manage Social Network Accounts.

Select Facebook and enter your account details to log in. For getting access to your Twitter account, go to the Social Network Accounts Setting screen, and either enter your account details or email address and password to connect.

Once again, even with these options, you can only share things on social media and not use Facebook and Twitter like they are used on a PC. In order to use these programs extensively, you can download the Facebook and Twitter apps from the Amazon App Store for free.

Email Set-Up

Now we will enable email settings on the Kindle. Unlock the screen and then scroll down from the top to bring the settings menu into view. Tap "More" and select "Applications. Next, select

"Email, Contacts, Calendars" to add an "Account.

You can simply type in the username and password for popular accounts, or enter in complete details for other accounts. This completes the set up for Email, Contacts, and Calendar events.

Working on the Home Screen

If you want to remove any item from the carrousel, long-press the icon to make the remove option appear.

You can also add items like apps, movies, Internet pages, and eBooks to favorites by long-pressing the icons and then tapping "Add to Favorites." The "favorites" icon is a star which you can find in the lower right of the screen. The icon provides quick access, especially when you are moving from one app or program to the other.

In addition, if you want to remove some apps from the favorites section, long-press the icon and select "Remove from favorites." Additionally, you can always rearrange the icons by long-pressing and then dragging them to the preferred location.

The Carousel

The carousel that you see on the main screen shows you all apps and programs that you have you used or viewed recently, such as books and videos. It is really simple to browse the carousel as you simply have to use a finger to view the items.

For selecting an item, simply tap it. But don't forget that items viewed recently will be shown first on the carousel. So if you have purchased something from Amazon, it will be displayed as "New." In addition, if you are reading an eBook, bookmark badges on the carousel can direct you where you left off.

Screen Rotation

Screen rotation has been enabled on the Kindle Fire HD by default. This means that the screen will turn to landscape or portrait mode; it depends how you are holding the tablet.

However, while reading an eBook or browsing the web, screen rotation can be irritating. To turn it off, swipe from the top of the screen to bring the "Notifications" screen into view. Next, tap the "Lock/Unlock" icon located at the upper left corner.

This can be done even in landscape or portrait mode. If you want to bring back rotation, simply tap the icon again.

Changing the Name

If you want to change the name on the upper left corner of the tablet, you need to sign in using your Amazon account and visiting the "Manage My Devices" page. You can then remove the default name and enter the name of your choice.

Camera Options

The Kindle Fire HD has a front-facing camera because the developers primarily have included it for video chat. If you want to use the camera, well, like a camera, you can download the PicShop Lite Photo Editor from the Amazon App Store for free. You can even upgrade to the paid version.

Once the app is installed, run it and tap the icon found at the lower left. Next, select "Camera" and you are good to go. However, even with

PicShop, you cannot record videos or capture panoramic images. We were surprised to note that there is a proper camera in the Kindle Fire HD, but it is "hidden "or at least that's what it seems like.

But overall this camera works fine. To open this application, you need the ES File Explorer. Once it is downloaded and installed, run the program and tap "AppMgr." You will find this icon in the upper right corner. Next, tap "Category", followed by "System Apps". Finally, tap the Camera icon.

The quality may not be superb, but this camera can help you record videos and take pictures, with zoom dial and other picture options. To attain focus, simply tap on the screen twice. However, there is no way currently to bring a camera icon to the main screen, which means you have to use ES Explorer every time to launch the camera.

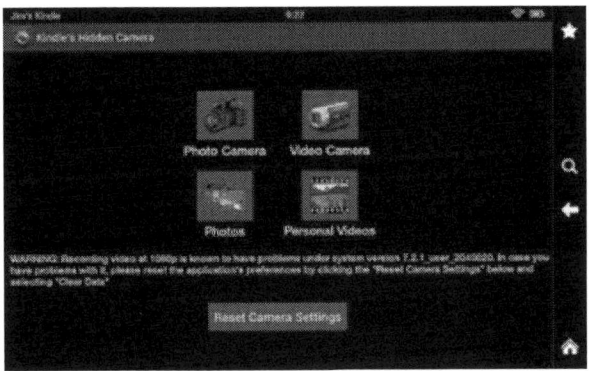

Bluetooth

Start by tuning on your Bluetooth device and your Kindle, via the settings menu. Tap "Wireless" followed by "Bluetooth" and "Enable. Tap the name of the device to bring it in view. Next, hit the name of the Bluetooth device which you are connecting the Kindle.

If the name does not show, then tap "search for devices." Don't worry about this. Chances are that you would have to connect the Bluetooth device again manually if you had turned it off for a while.

Micro HDMI Cables

As mentioned at the opening of these eBook, the new Kindle Fire HD comes with micro a HDMI port through which you can connect the tablet to the TV or a monitor. Of course, you will require special cables for this purpose, which can be easily found on Amazon, costing hardly a few bucks. You can even purchase an adaptor ("Micro-Type D) to fit a full size cable connector.

Downloading Music from Cloud

If you have created a music collection on Amazon's cloud drive, you can download or stream it on your Kindle. Amazon allows streaming or downloading of 250 songs for free. If you want to add more songs, there is a $24.99 program which offers more than 250,000 songs.

Remote Access

Download the Splashtop Remote Android app to access your computer files and programs directly on your tablet. This way you can work even when a PC is not available.

Text Options

Some apps and programs, such as the web browser, require that you select, copy, and paste some text. You can do this by long pressing a word and then dragging the tiny arrows. To paste the selected text, long-press in the entry field where you want to enter the text, and the option for pasting will appear.

Similar components exist for links and images on the web browser as well; long pressing can bring up saving, sharing, and other options.

Google Maps

Google Maps are a great program that is useful for finding new and alternate routes and avoiding traffic. Street View also works well along the same lines. However, both these applications are missing from the Kindle tablets.

However, you can always side load them from various 3rd party websites, and these versions work pretty well.

Removing Ads

Ads are one of the most annoying features of the Kindle Fire HD. The problem is that they cannot be removed directly from the tablet. Here is how you go about it.

Begin by logging in your Amazon.com account, and then go to "Manage Your Kindle" page under "My Account.

In the "Your Kindle Account" section, choose "Manage your Devices", where you will find the list of all the devices linked to your account. Click "Edit" found under "Special Offers." Here you can cancel all offers and screen-saver ads on your tablet.

Note: If you can spend $15 to remove the ads, click "Unsubscribe Now".

Preserving the Battery

Nothing is more annoying than a dead battery just when you are fully immersed in your tablet. In this section, we will teach you how to keep an eye on your battery usage, along with some tips

to make the best use of your battery.

How to Check Battery Percentage

To view the battery usage, go to settings and select "Device.

An App for Monitoring the Battery

For a better way to monitor your battery's charge, you can download the GSam Battery Monitor app. One of the best features of this app is that the exact battery % will be given to you via notifications, which means you do not have to open the settings menu every time.

Turn Wi-Fi Off When Not in Use

One of the best methods of preserving battery life is to disconnect the Wi-Fi when you are not using it. This can be done easily by tapping the gears icon located at the top bar. The quick access makes turning Wi-Fi on/off easy.

Good App Selection

Sometimes an app can suck all the battery power of the tablet. The GSam battery app mentioned above (also known as the Badass Battery Monitor) will show you a list of the all the apps you are using along with their battery usage. After installing the app, launch it and then select "app usage" to view the list of apps.

The Monthly Charge Cycle

The monthly charge cycle is a simple yet highly potent technique of knowing your battery's running time and quality, especially on lithium ion batteries. Here is how you perform the cycle.

Once in a month, completely drain the battery and after that leave to it to charge fully. Performing this task every month will prolong your battery's performance in the long-run. You can even set up a reminder to avoid forgetting it.

Watch Out For Temperature

Another aspect of lithium ion batteries is that they are susceptible to high temperatures, and if they are constantly kept in such temperatures, they will be damaged for good sooner or later. Try always to store your Kindle in room temperature.

Cooler temperatures are more bearable. If the device is lying in a cool temperature, the battery life can reduce in the short-run, but once the device finds itself in a warmer environment, the battery performance will return to normal.

Adjust the Brightness

This one is simple to understand. When you do not require high brightness, you can always decrease to save some battery usage. Just like the Wi-Fi, you can quickly adjust the brightness from the settings toolbar.

Tap the icon for settings in the top bar. You will see a slider, which can be moved to increase or decrease brightness. Of course, when you are reducing brightness, adjust to a ratio that goes

easy on your eyesight.

Keeping an Eye on Memory

Viewing Memory

Most Kindle Fire HD features can be viewed in the settings menu. To see how much memory you have left, open the settings menu (swipe down from the top).

Extra Memory

For the most part, the built-in memory is all that users require. Nevertheless, if you still require extra memory, remember that Kindle Fire HD has no provision for an SD card, and you will have to purchase it additionally.

The good news is that the Kindle allows for cloud storage if you want to save additional files and documents.

Some of the best cloud programs you can use on the Kindle Fire HD include Dropbox and SugarSync.

Note that cloud storage on Kindle Fire HD is free up to a 5 GB limit, after which you have to pay for extra storage.

Additional Tips

Conversion of eBook files will be discussed later, but for now it is useful to note that converting your eBooks using the Calibre program reduces the Mobipocket or simply MOBI file in size. So even if you don't have slots for expanding memory on Kindle Fire, effective techniques like converting eBooks can save a lot of storage space on the tablet.

Enhance the eBook Reading Experience

You don't really need to improve the reading experience on the new Kindle Fire HD, as it is better than on the previous versions. The tighter pixels help the screen to come close to a "Retina" display where dots connecting the pixels cannot be spotted.

In addition, if you prefer reading at night, you will feel less strain on your eyes as the devices turns dimmer.

In this section, you will learn some tips to make your reading experience on Kindle Fire HD.

Dimming the Screen

It is quite possible that while reading at the night the lowest brightness would still be high for some people. This can be adjusted with the help of a screen filter.

Reading ePub eBooks on Kindle Fire HD

You can easily find ePub reading apps on Amazon, but they have not been featured on the Kindle Fire HD. However, you can always side load other reading apps such as Aldiko, Nook, and Kobo.

If you want to ePub books on the tablet, you can to convert the ePub files into a Kindle Fire HD compatible format. One of the simplest ways to do this is to download Calibre.

This is an eBook management program. You can download it on your Linux, Mac, or Windows system, and then plug in your Kindle. ePub files will be converted as you add them to your device. In addition, Calibre can also convert PDF files.

Setting up Calibre is easy after you download it. Accept the license, click install, and then leave the final set-up screen as it is. Once the program is installed, simply click "Add Books" to attach ePub books to Calibre. Browse the folder where the books are listed to add them.

Now connect your tablet to the PC and once it is recognized, you will see an icon appear at the top of the program titled "Send to Device." Click to highlight all files you want to send to the tablet and then click the icon.

An option for auto-conversion will pop-up on which you have to click "Yes." On the bottom-right of the screen you can see the status of the conversion. Once it reaches zero, you can safely disconnect the device.

Note: You require a micro-USB data cable to transfer files to the tablet. This data cable does not come with the device.

Reading Nook Books on Kindle Fire HD

If you have previously used Nook for reading eBooks, you will feel a little disappointed while reading using the Kindle Fire HD as it does not support the ePub format. We have already learnt how to convert ePub files to Kindle Fire format (TXT, MOBI, AZW) through Calibre.

However, as useful it is, this conversion procedure takes a lot of time, especially if you want to keep all your eBooks in sync with your devices. In addition, the majority of eBooks in the Nook format have DRM protection, and Calibre does not support DRM conversion.

That is why you will have to download the Nook app on the Kindle Fire HD. You can even install download using third-party websites like GetJar. After installing GetJar on your device, simply search for it in the app library and use it to find Nook.

You can also use Dropbox to install the Nook app on your system and transfer it into the tablet.

Listing eBooks as "Books"

We have talked about "side loading" a collection of eBooks on the Kindle Fire. If you have already executed this technique, you must have noticed that the transferred files show up as "Docs" instead of "Books."

However, listing eBooks under "Books" allows you to search for a title by author name, which is useful if you have an extensive collection. To list your eBooks as "Books", set up Calibre and select files for transfer. Be sure to keep MOBI as the output format.

Next, click on MOBI Output (left column) and cross out a tag (PDOC) in the "Personal Doc tag" section. To remove this tag for good, go to "Preferences" and select "Output Options." Go to "MOBI Output" and remove the tag permanently.

Hit "OK" to begin conversion. Once the files are converted, copy them to the "Books" folder on your tablet.

Non-Amazon eBooks and Personal Documents

You can easily download non-Amazon eBooks and other documents on your Fire by using the "send to Kindle" app. Alternately, you can email these files to Kindle Fire's free email address, which you can find under "My Account" in the settings menu. You can change this address in the personal documents settings on the "Manage Your Kindle" page.

Library Books

You can easily download free eBooks that you download from your local library. Alternately, you can use the OverDrive app for this purpose.

Keep Away from Kids!

The Internet is not a safe place for children, and if they get access to your credit store, it can turn into a nightmare for you! And now since the Internet is available on devices like the Kindle Fire that kids can pick up easily (and finger their way around), all concerned parents should take some steps to ensure nothing harmful results from the innocent behavior.

This is not just for protecting the children from sexually explicit or violent content. Many viral videos on the Internet use cartoon characters and dub in adult content.

Parental Controls

In the settings menu of your Kindle Fire, there is an option for parental controls. Here you can enter a password which restricts the purchase of content along with access to the web browser, specific apps, and more. So even if by accident a child finds your device, he/she will not be able to enter into restricted territory.

Securing Wi-Fi

The Kindle Fire has an option for users to lock the Wi-Fi with a password. This will secure the web browser, email, and credit card connected Amazon account. On the other hand, there is a host of children's eBook, games, movies, and cartoons that can be viewed on the Kindle Fire

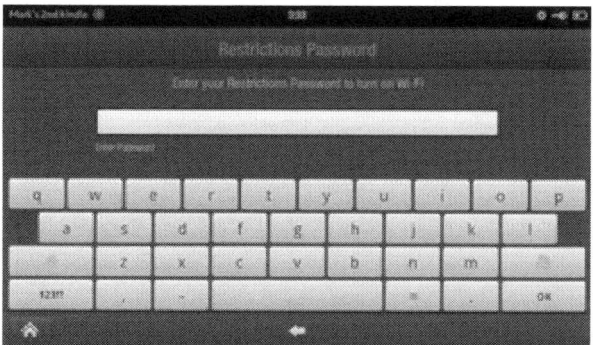

HD without Wi-Fi access.

All About Apps

In this section, we will list down some tips for downloading and using apps on the Kindle Fire HD.

Installing apps on the Kindle is easy, as you simply have to browse and download apps from the Amazon App Store, which will begin automatically when the tablet is connected to a Wi-Fi network. Automatic updates are enabled on the Kindle Fire HD, which means the latest versions of your apps will be installed automatically.

You will only receive a notification that the app has been updated. If you have disabled this option, you will have to grant permission every time an update is installed. To disable the updates, go to the settings menu and select

"Automatic updates. Uncheck the box beside "Enable Automatic Updates" to disable updates.

3rd Party Apps

To install apps from outside the Amazon store, you have to go to the settings menu, and select "Device Turn on "Allow Installation of Applications from Unknown sources." We have already mentioned GetJar and Imobile, but there are several 3rd party app platforms that you can access, such as SlideMe, Opera Mobile App Store, Soc.io Mall, and Android Freeware.

This goes without saying: you need to exercise caution while downloading apps from a 3rd party source to avoid the threat of malware.

Free App of the Day

Be sure to visit the Amazon App Store every day or as regularly as possible to check out the free android app of the day.

Side loading Apps

There are various methods of side loading apps. For instance, you can keep the apk files in internal memory of the tablet, and then locate them using the file manager. Tap a certain app to initiate installation.

Or, as mentioned before, you can Dropbox for file storage. So when you use the tablet's web browser to download the apps, simply tap a file once (after it has downloaded) to begin installation.

Note: The Kindle Fire does not come with file management software, which means you have to download one yourself. One of the best programs in this regard is the ES File Explorer which can be downloaded for free from Amazon.

Using YouTube

You can use YouTube with the Silk web browser on the tablet. This web browser re-formats the content of a specific webpage to provide a clearer view. There are a various options for formatting, along with different text sizes.

Note that the silk reader only appears on article-type pages. You can find this in the web browser tab through the green glasses icon.

However, a better option is to side load the YouTube app will also help you enjoy videos, even in HD. However, you cannot login on a side loaded app.

Free Calculator Apps

Of course, you will usually not use the Kindle Fire HD for working out mathematics. But sometimes you need a calculator for tasks like online shopping and a calculator app within the device comes in handy. The Kindle Fire HD does not have a built-in calculator, but you can also download one from the Amazon App Store for free.

App Notifications

Although notifications are a useful feature, they can sometimes irritate you. To avoid this, you can always turn off notifications for individual apps. Go to "Settings" and select "Applications." You can turn off app notifications in "Notification Settings."

Giving Your Kindle Away

Of course you will continue using your Kindle Fire HD for a while. But just in case you are planning to sell or present it to someone else, there are some preparations that need to be made.

To begin with, ensure that all personal and account information has been erased, which means resetting the device back to factory settings. However, you would naturally want to retain some important files, because once you reset the device, the files are history. In addition, if those files have been side loaded, getting them is much more difficult than re-downloading Amazon apps.

It is also important to check your battery life since resetting requires at least 40% charging. If you are charging the battery, keep it a few points above 40% just to be on the safe side.

Once you have charged the battery, go back to "Device" settings. Scroll down and tap "Reset to Factory Defaults" followed by "Erase everything." Doing so will cancel your registration at Amazon. The device will reboot, which takes a couple of minutes.

Your passwords and all other personal information will now be deleted and you can give

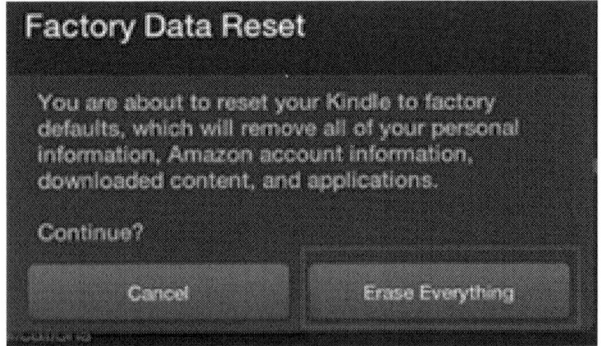

your tablet away without any worries.

Conclusion

That's all for now. By this time, you should be navigating the Kindle Fire HD smoothly, all the while enjoying its exciting features. We have been careful in adding only those tips that would really help you make the most of your device, and nothing would please us more than seeing you enjoy the features of your Kindle Fire without any difficulty.

32860552R00027

Made in the USA
Lexington, KY
04 June 2014